The Fruit Group

by Helen Frost

Consulting Editor: Gail Saunders-Smith, Ph.D.

Consultant: Linda Hathaway
Health Educator
McMillen Center for Health Education

Pebble Books

an imprint of Capstone Press
Mankato, Minnesota

Pebble Books are published by Capstone Press
151 Good Counsel Drive, P.O. Box 669, Mankato, Minnesota 56002
http://www.capstone-press.com

1 2 3 4 5 6 05 04 03 02 01 00

Library of Congress Cataloging-in-Publication Data
Frost, Helen, 1949–
    The fruit group/by Helen Frost.
    p.cm.—(Food guide pyramid)
    Includes bibliographical references and index.
    Summary: Simple text and photographs present the foods that are part of the
fruit group and their nutritional importance.
    ISBN 0-7368-0537-0
    1. Nutrition—Juvenile literature. 2. Fruit—Juvenile literature. [1. Fruit.
2. Nutrition.] I. Title. II. Series.
TX355.F767   2000
613.2—dc21
                                                                    99-047739

Note to Parents and Teachers

The Food Guide Pyramid series supports national science standards
related to physical health and nutrition. This book describes and
illustrates the fruit group. The photographs support early readers
in understanding the text. The repetition of words and phrases
helps early readers learn new words. This book also introduces
early readers to subject-specific vocabulary words, which are
defined in the Words to Know section. Early readers may need
assistance to read some words and to use the Table of Contents,
Words to Know, Read More, Internet Sites, and Index/Word List
sections of the book.

Table of Contents

The food guide pyramid shows the foods you need to stay healthy. The fruit group is near the bottom of the food guide pyramid.

seeds

A fruit is a part of
a plant that people
eat. A fruit has seeds.

Apples are in
the fruit group.

Bananas are in
the fruit group.

Grapes are in
the fruit group.

Strawberries are in
the fruit group.

Oranges are in
the fruit group.

Fruit juice is in
the fruit group.

You need two to four servings of fruit every day. Fruit gives your body energy and helps you stay healthy.

Words to Know

energy—the strength to be active without becoming tired; eating fruit gives you energy.

food guide pyramid—a triangle split into six areas to show the different foods people need; a pyramid is big at the bottom and small at the top; people need more food from the bottom of the food guide pyramid than from the top.

fruit—the fleshy, juicy part of a plant that people eat; fruits have seeds.

healthy—fit and well; fruit has nutrients that help you stay healthy.

serving—a helping of food or drink; one serving from the fruit group is one piece of fruit about the size of a tennis ball, a melon wedge, 3/4 cup (175 ml) of juice, 1/2 cup (125 ml) of canned fruit, or 1/4 cup (50 ml) of dried fruit.

Read More

Bryant-Mole, Karen. *Food.* Picture This! Crystal Lake, Ill.: Rigby, 1997.

Frost, Helen. *Eating Right.* The Food Guide Pyramid. Mankato, Minn.: Pebble Books, 2000.

Kalbacken, Joan. *The Food Pyramid.* A True Book. New York: Children's Press, 1998.

Powell, Jillian. *Fruit.* Everyone Eats. Austin, Texas: Raintree Steck-Vaughn, 1997.

Internet Sites

The Food Guide Pyramid
http://kidshealth.org/kid/food/pyramid.html

Food Guide Pyramid Game
http://www.nppc.org/cgi-bin/pyramid

Fruit and Vegetable Encyclopedia: Bananas
http://www.dole5aday.com/encyclopedia/
banana/banana_menu.html

Index/Word List

Word Count: 96
Early-Intervention Level: 8

Editorial Credits

Mari C. Schuh, editor; Heather Kindseth, cover designer; Sara A. Sinnard, illustrator;
   Kia Bielke, illustrator; Kimberly Danger, photo researcher

Photo Credits

International Stock/L. J. Schneider, 1; Dusty Willison, 20
Craig Lovell, cover
Kim Stanton, 12
Lawrence Sawyer/Index Stock Imagery, 8
Mark Turner, 14
Photo Agora, 18
Photophile, 10
PNI/© DigitalVision, 6
Visuals Unlimited/Inga Spence, 16